Going to S

Written by Nicholas Spencer

You can ride on a bus
to school.

These four children
ride on a bus.

You can ride in a car
to school.

These five children
ride in a car.

You can walk
to school.

These six children walk.

How do you go to school?

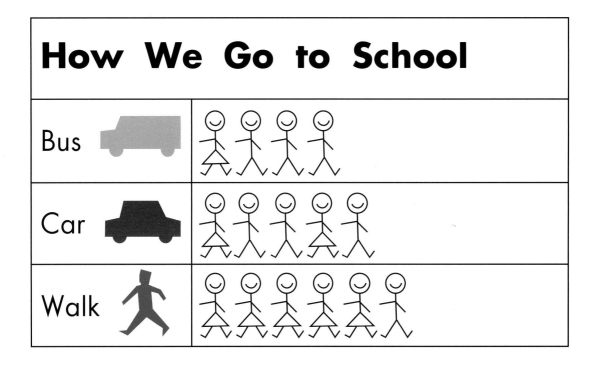

How We Go to School

Bus		
Car		
Walk		